D1519996

PHONES

100 YEARS AGO

by Allison Lassieur

amicus readers 2

amicus readers

Say hello to amicus readers.

You'll find our helpful dog, Amicus, chasing a ball—to let you know the reading level of a book.

A

1

2

Learn to Read
Frequent repetition of sentence structures, high frequency words, and familiar topics provide ample support for brand new readers. Approximately 100 words.

Read Independently
Repetition is mixed with varied sentence structures and 6 to 8 content words per book are introduced with photo label and picture glossary supports. Approximately 150 words.

Read to Know More
These books feature a higher text load with additional nonfiction features such as more photos, time lines, and text divided into sections. Approximately 250 words.

Amicus Readers are published by Amicus
P.O. Box 1329, Mankato, Minnesota 56002
www.amicuspublishing.us

U.S. publication copyright © 2012 Amicus.
International copyright reserved in all countries.
No part of this book may be reproduced in any form without written permission from the publisher.

Printed in the United States of America at Corporate Graphics, in North Mankato, Minnesota.

Series Editor   Rebecca Glaser
Series Designer   Heather Dreisbach
Photo Researcher   Heather Dreisbach

Library of Congress Cataloging-in-Publication Data
Lassieur, Allison.
   Phones : 100 years ago / by Allison Lassieur.
      p. cm. – (Amicus Readers. 100 years ago)
   Includes index.
   Summary: "Discusses turn-of-the-century telephones and how they looked and worked much differenlty from the early 1900s to today. Includes "What's Different?" photo quiz"-Provided by publisher.
   ISBN 978-1-60753-165-4 (library binding)
   1. Telephone–History–Juvenile literature. I. Title.
TK6015.L37 2012
621.385-dc22
                                      2010039110

Photo Credits
Vintage Images/Alamy, cover, 9; H. Armstrong Roberts, 1, 20m; INTERFOTO/Alamy, 4; Stefano Bianchetti/Corbis, 5, 20b; Jack Benton/Getty Images, 6; L. W. HARRIS/National Geographic Stock, 7, 20t, 21t; Brand X Pictures/Getty Images, 10; DEA/A. DAGLI ORTI/Getty Images, 11; Bettmann/CORBIS, 12, 14; Buyenlarge/Getty Images, 13, 21m; John Jenkins/Spark Museum, 16; FPG/Getty Images, 17; ClassicStock/Alamy, 18; The Print Collector/Photolibrary, 21b, 22t

1024   3-2011
10 9 8 7 6 5 4 3 2 1

TABLE OF CONTENTS

Hello? The First Telephones   4

Different Kinds of Phones   6

Making a Call   12

Pay Phones   16

Photo Glossary   20

What's Different?   22

Ideas for Parents and Teachers   23

Index and Web Sites   24

Hello?
The First Telephones

Alexander Graham Bell invented the telephone more than one hundred years ago, in 1876. By the early 1900s, telephones were part of daily life.

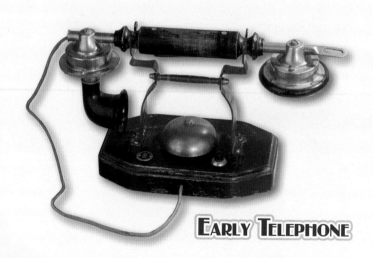

EARLY TELEPHONE

ALEXANDER GRAHAM BELL

DIFFERENT KINDS OF PHONES

The most common phones were called "candlestick" telephones. They were tall and thin like candlesticks.

People talked into the round
mouthpiece on the top. They put
the earpiece to their ear to listen.

Wooden wall telephones were shaped like boxes. They had nicknames like "coffin" and "fiddleback." The mouthpiece and the earpiece were separate. The caller turned a crank to make a call. The cord was short. Anyone who talked on these phones had to stand near the phone.

Desk phones were called cradle telephones. The receiver rested in the "cradle." The receiver had a handle with both an earpiece and a mouthpiece.

MAKING A CALL

One hundred years ago, most phones didn't have dials or buttons. The caller picked up the receiver and spoke to an operator.

Most operators were women.
Telephone companies thought women
had nicer voices than men.

Every call lit up a button on a big electronic switchboard. The operator plugged in cords and flipped switches to connect the call. Most calls were not private. Many families shared one phone line, called a "party line."

Pay Phones

Pay phones had coin slots for nickels, dimes, and quarters. After someone made a call, the operator told the caller how much to pay.

Sometimes there was only one phone in a whole town. The phone was usually near the general store. Everyone in town used it. Today it is hard to imagine life without a telephone.

Photo Glossary

candlestick telephone— a telephone in the shape of a tall, thin candle holder

earpiece—the part of a telephone that the caller listens from

invent—to create something new that has not been thought of before

mouthpiece—the part of a telephone the caller talks into

operator—a person who works at a phone company and helps connect phone calls

switchboard—the control center or panel for connecting the lines of a telephone system

WHAT'S DIFFERENT?

How many differences can you find between the phone companies from 1910 and from today? What is the same?

Ideas for Parents and Teachers

100 Years Ago, an Amicus Readers Level 2 series, introduces children to everyday life about 100 years ago, in the early 1900s. Use the following strategies to help readers predict and comprehend the text.

Before Reading
- Ask the child about telephones and communication.
- Have him or her describe how the phone is a part of daily life.
- Ask about the things that a modern phone can do.

Read the Book
- Read the book to the child, or have him or her read it independently.
- Point out details in the photos that are interesting or new to the child.
- Show the child how to interpret the photos and how the images relate to the text.

After Reading
- Have the child explain how telephones changed the lives of people.
- Encourage the child to think further by asking questions such as, *How easy was it to communicate with friends and family then?* and *What would it have been like to live in a house with no telephone?*

23

INDEX

Alexander Graham Bell	4	party line	15
candlestick phone	6	pay phones	16, 17
cords	8, 15	receiver	11, 12
cradle telephones	11	switchboard	15
earpiece	7, 8, 11	telephone companies	13
mouthpiece	7, 8, 11	wall telephones	8
operators	12, 13, 15, 16, 17		

WEB SITES

History of the Telephone for Kids
http://www.fcc.gov/cgb/kidszone/history_telephone.html

Library of Congress: Who Really Invented the Telephone?
http://www.loc.gov/rr/scitech/mysteries/telephone.html

Telephone History
http://www.telephonymuseum.com/history.htm